The First Book of Broadway Solos

Compiled by Joan Frey Boytim

T0053165

HAL•LEONARD®
CORPORATION
7777 W. BLUEMOUND RD. P.O. BOX 13819 MILWAUKEE, WI 53213

Visit Hal Leonard Online at
www.halleonard.com

Preface

When a beginning student of voice is ready for song literature, it is very important that some musical theatre material be included in the lesson repertoire. (This comment applies to American, Canadian, British, or other native English-speaking students.) Show tunes are a unique American and British contribution to the music world. Many of them are very useful for developing a smooth vocal line in an idiom that speaks to teenagers and new adult students. Not only is the music very melodic, the fact that the words are in a student's native language is an enormous advantage. *The First Book of Broadway Solos* attempts to address a traditional, classical voice teacher's sensibilities and needs in teaching basic techniques of singing.

The frustrations that I have experienced as a teacher are: (1) the vocal selection books from individual shows have, at most, two or three suitable songs for a particular voice; (2) the many piano/vocal show tune collections available have only several songs in good vocal study keys (mezzo-soprano being the exception); (3) the editions of songs taken from the actual vocal scores found in excellent publications such as *The Singer's Musical Theatre Anthology* are, in many cases, unsuitable for the beginning student because they are too long, too involved, and often in difficult keys for the novice singer.

The songs selected for *The First Book of Broadway Solos* were chosen for use by beginning voice students to assist in developing a solid vocal technique during the first several months or years of lessons. In most cases, the original voice category is preserved, although at times I chose, for musical and vocal reasons, to use a song originally sung by a baritone or tenor, for instance, in the mezzo-soprano collection (of course, taking into account the suitability of the text). Many keys have been altered to accommodate the ranges of the majority of teenagers and beginning adult students using these books. For those persons coming from a theatre point of view, it should be noted that these books are not designed for the belting style of singing. Specifically, mezzo-soprano is classically defined in this series (rather than the definition of this voice type by the theatre world as a belter). That is not to say that a more theatrical style of singing is not important or needed in other contexts. For the purposes of vocal instruction, classically based, lyric singing is the aim of this series.

Because many of the standard show tunes tend to be too low for the developing soprano voice, the majority of the keys in that volume have been raised. Most of the songs focus on a modest range comfortable for beginning singers, although several songs will showcase those students who are developing a higher vocal range. Many of the original keys, as published in the vocal selections of a show, were retained for the mezzo-soprano volume. More than half of the keys in the tenor collection have been raised to meet the vocal needs of the higher male voice. In most cases, the ranges in the baritone/bass volume have been lowered because the typical beginning baritone or bass struggles with the upper range tessitura and occasional high notes. A few of the songs were transposed down for the true bass range.

All the books include a few vocally challenging pieces, as well as a few more unfamiliar and unique entries. Overall, the songs in these four volumes include a wide variety of classics representative of the last seventy-five years of Broadway shows.

It is my hope that the studio voice teacher or the high school choral director will find this series a valuable resource, providing students with literature that is teachable, fun, and is an excellent introduction to the unique art form of musical theatre.

Joan Frey Boytim

The First Book of Broadway Solos

Compiled by Joan Frey Boytim

* Off-Broadway

BRING HIM HOME

LES MISÉRABLES

Music by CLAUDE-MICHEL SCHÖNBERG
Lyrics by HERBERT KRETZMER and ALAIN BOUBLIL

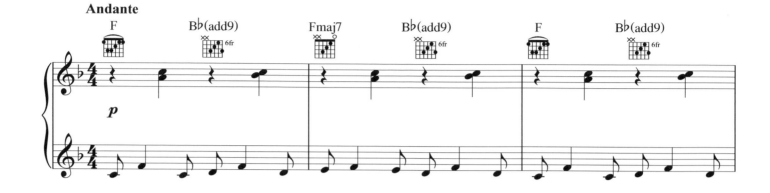

God on high, _____ hear my
peace, _____ bring him

prayer. _____ In my need _____ You have
joy. _____ He is young, _____ he is

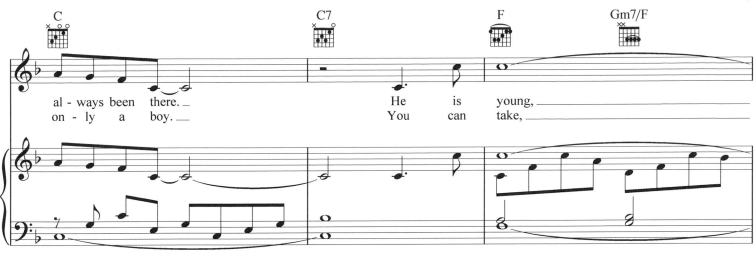

al - ways been there.___ He is young,___
on - ly a boy.___ You can take,___

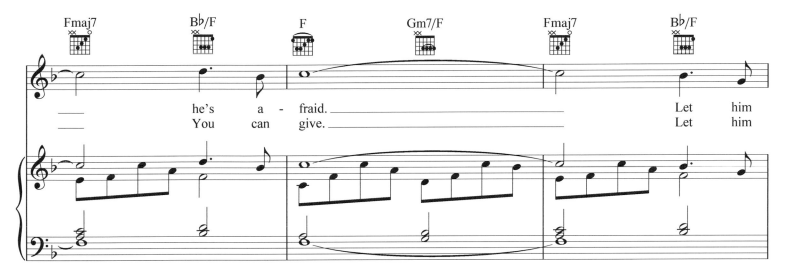

___ he's a - fraid.___ Let him
___ You can give.___ Let him

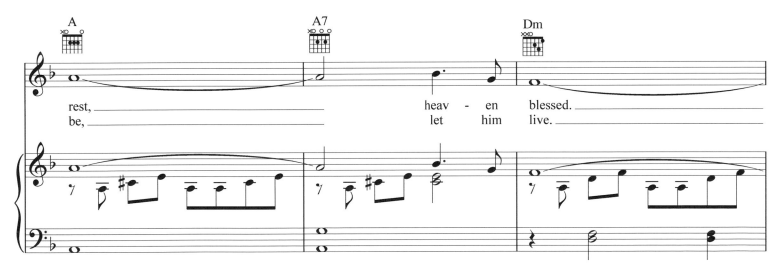

rest,___ heav - en blessed.
be,___ let him live.

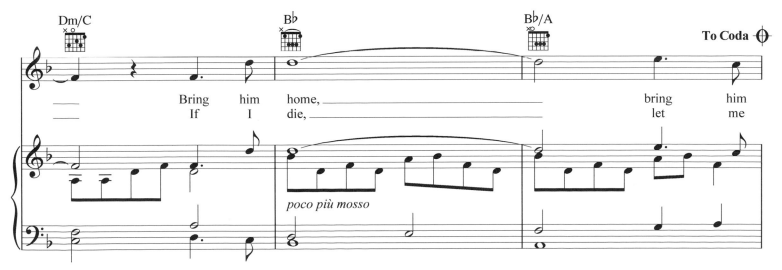

___ Bring him home, bring him
___ If I die, let me

poco più mosso

To Coda ⊕

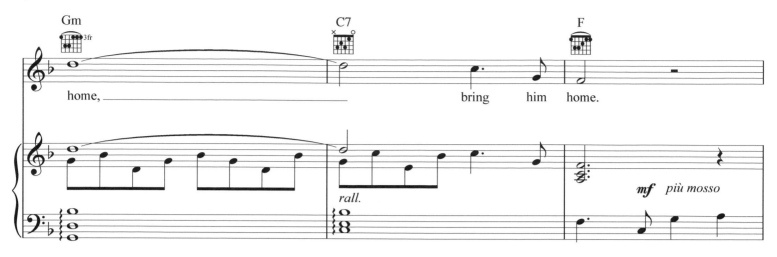

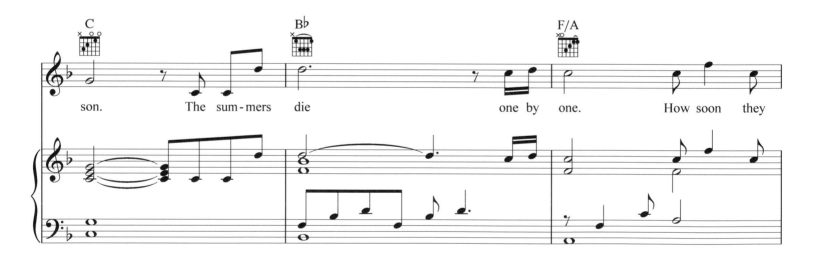

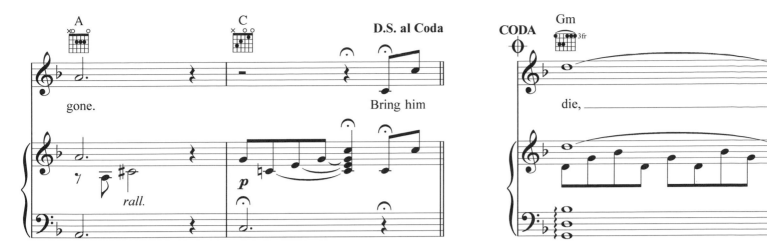

gone.

D.S. al Coda

Bring him

CODA

die, _____

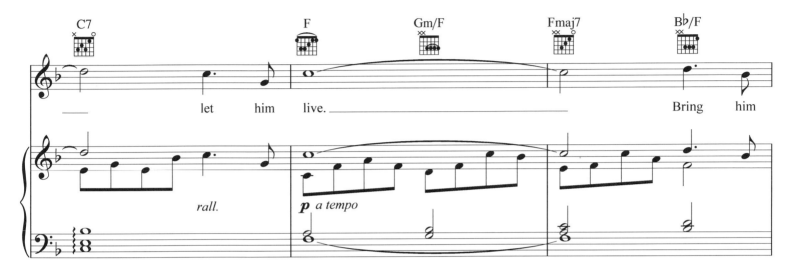

let him live. _____ Bring him

rall.

p a tempo

home, _____ bring him home, _____ bring him

dim. _rall. molto_

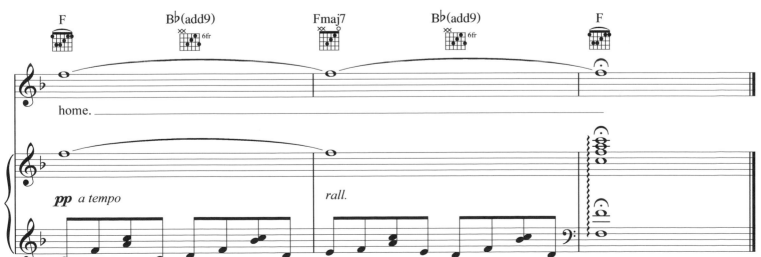

home. _____

pp a tempo

rall.

I BELIEVE IN YOU
HOW TO SUCCEED IN BUSINESS WITHOUT REALLY TRYING

By FRANK LOESSER

Note: Finch is addressing himself in the song.

religioso e molto legato

Oh, I be - lieve in you, _____

I be - lieve in you. _____ *with self-assurance* I hear the

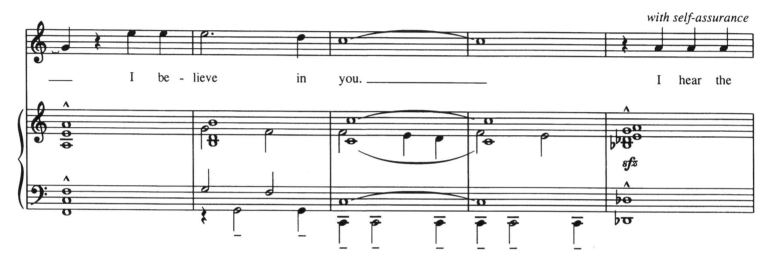

sound of good, sol - id judg - ment when - ev - er you

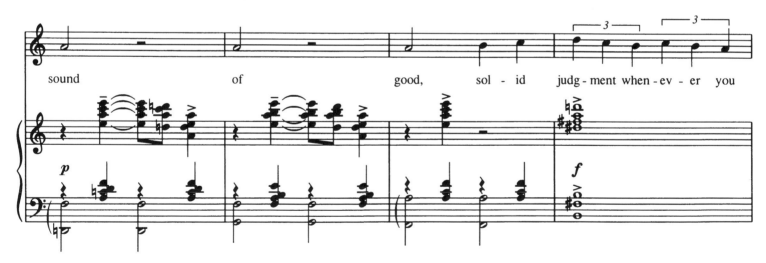

talk; Yet, there's the bold,

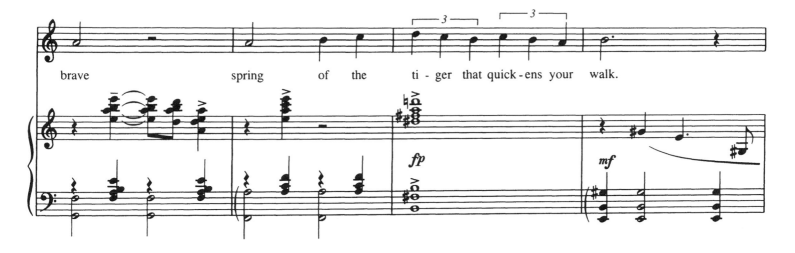

brave   spring   of   the   ti - ger that quick - ens your walk.

religioso e molto legato

Oh, I be - lieve   in   you, _____

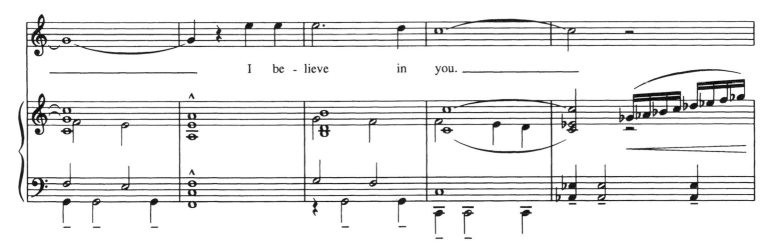

_____ I be - lieve   in   you. _____

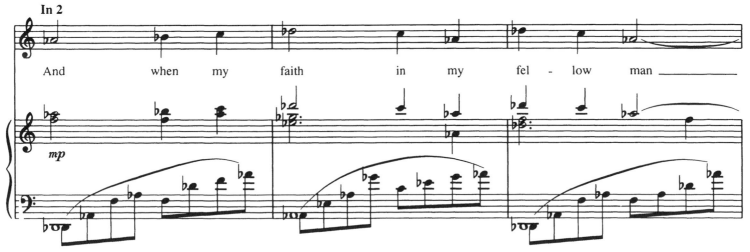

In 2

And   when   my   faith   in   my   fel - low   man _____

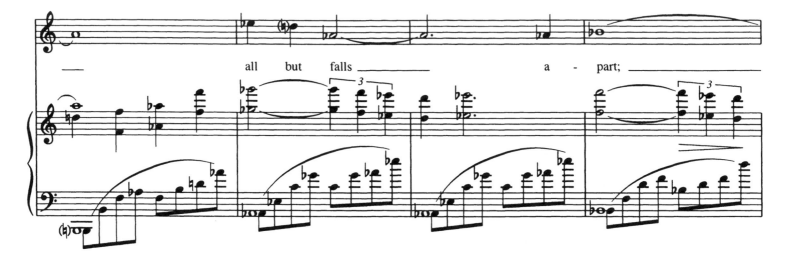

all but falls   a - part;

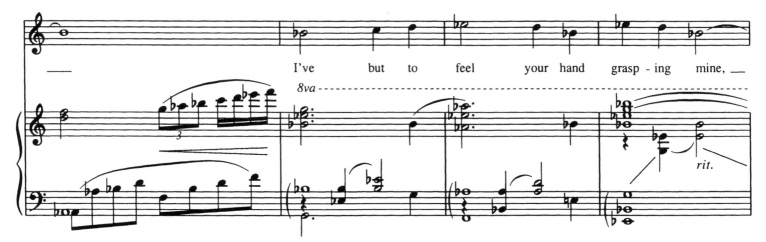

I've but to feel your hand grasp - ing mine,   *rit.*

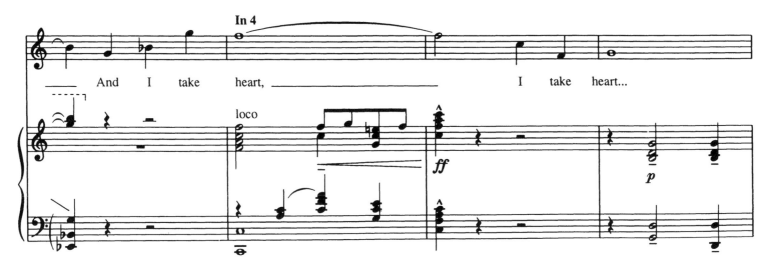

And I take heart,   I take heart...

ten.   ten.   ten.   **A tempo**

To see the cool,   clear   eyes of a

seek-er of wis-dom and truth;   Yet, with the

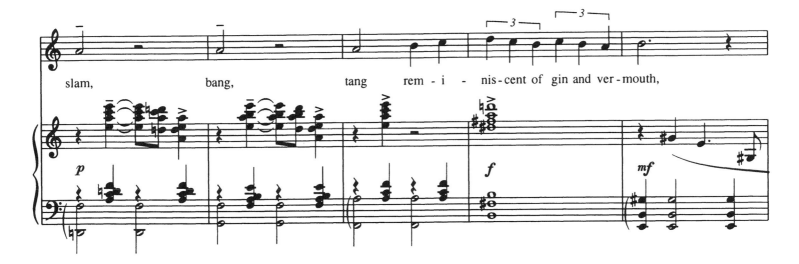

slam,   bang,   tang rem - i - nis-cent of gin and ver-mouth,

religioso e molto legato

Oh, I be - lieve   in you, _____

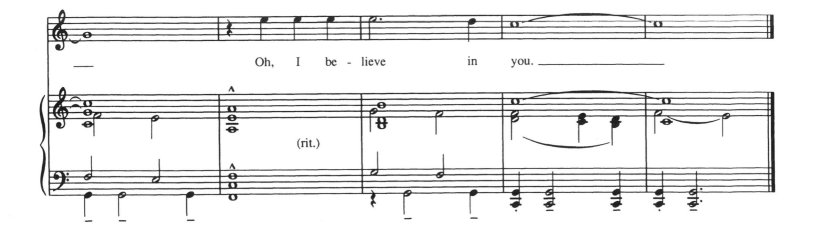

Oh, I be - lieve   in you. _____

(rit.)

I COULD WRITE A BOOK

PAL JOEY

Words by LORENZ HART
Music by RICHARD RODGERS

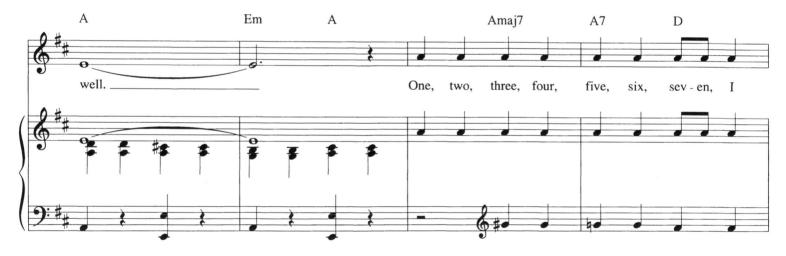

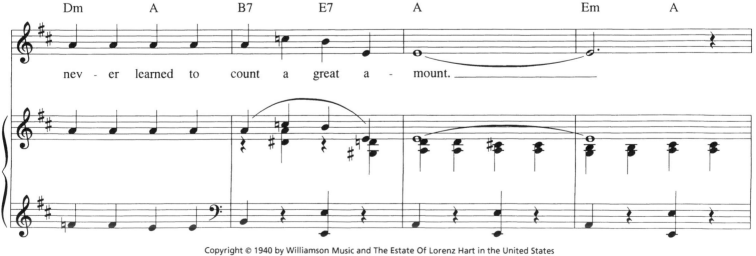

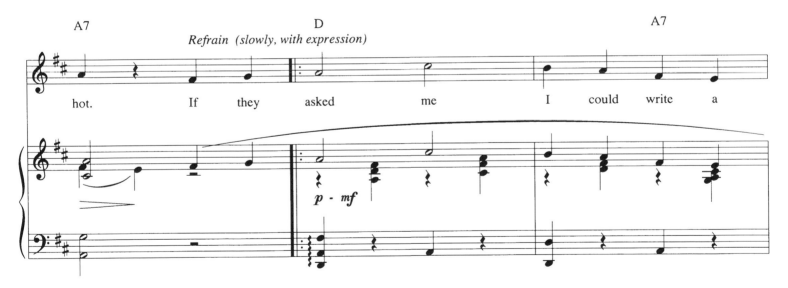

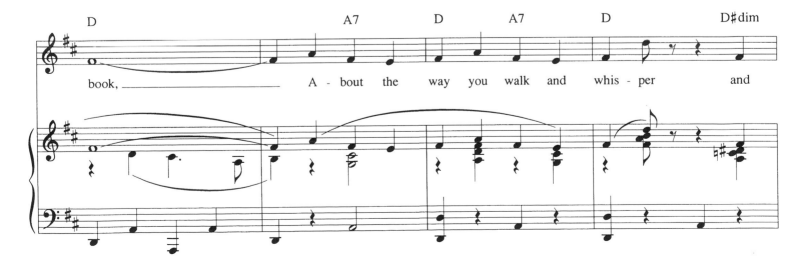

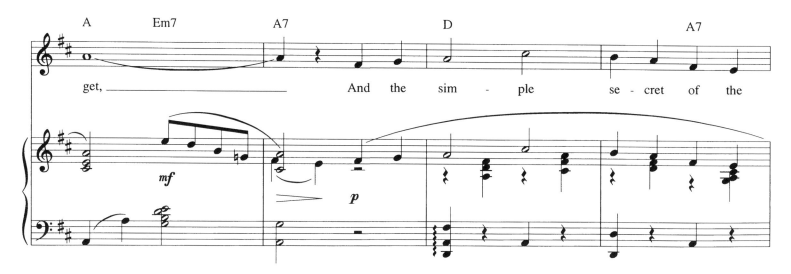

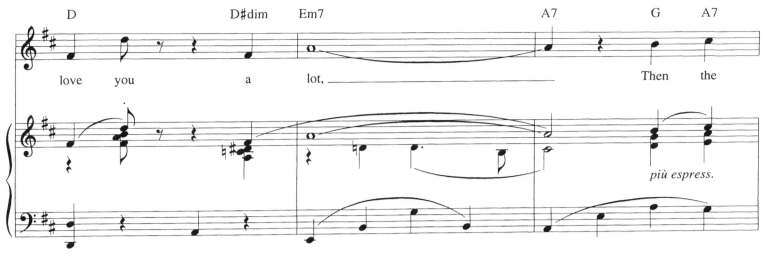

love you a lot, _____ Then the

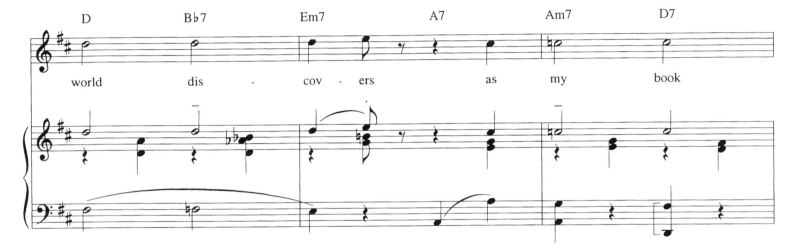

world dis - cov - ers as my book

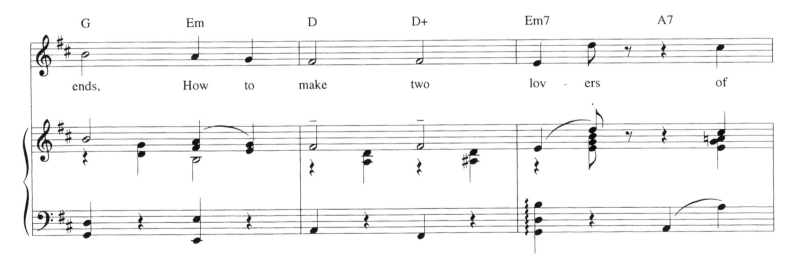

ends, How to make two lov - ers of

friends. If they friends. _____

I DO NOT KNOW A DAY I DID NOT LOVE YOU

TWO BY TWO

Lyrics by MARTIN CHARNIN
Music by RICHARD RODGERS

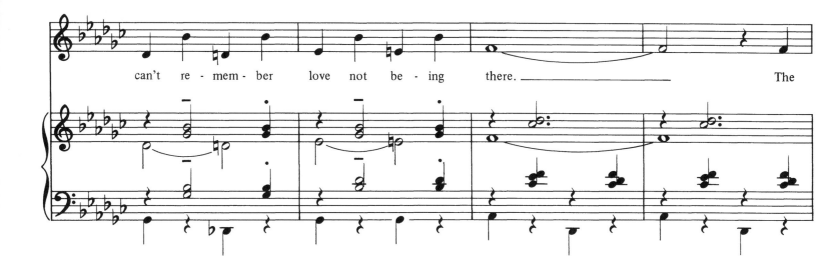

har - vest when the sun danced in your hair. _____ I

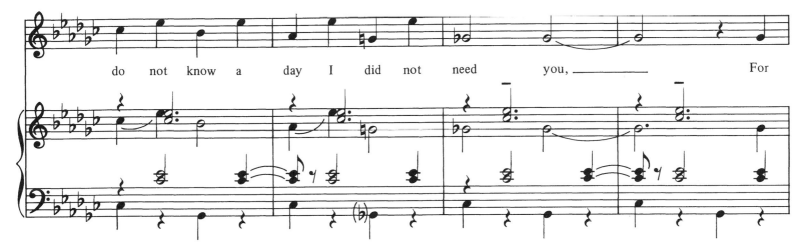

do not know a day I did not need you, _____ For

shar - ing ev - 'ry mo - ment that I spent. _____ I

need - ed you be - fore I ev - er knew you, _____ Be - fore I

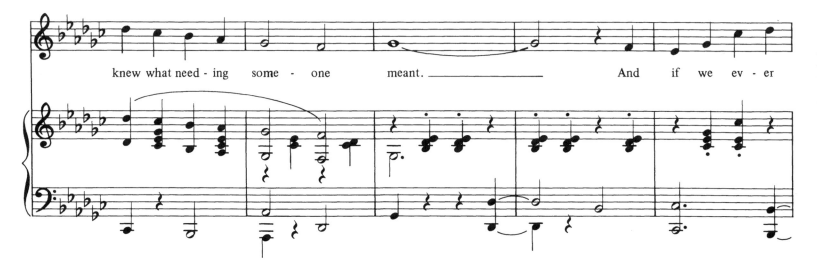

knew what need-ing some-one meant. _____ And if we ev-er

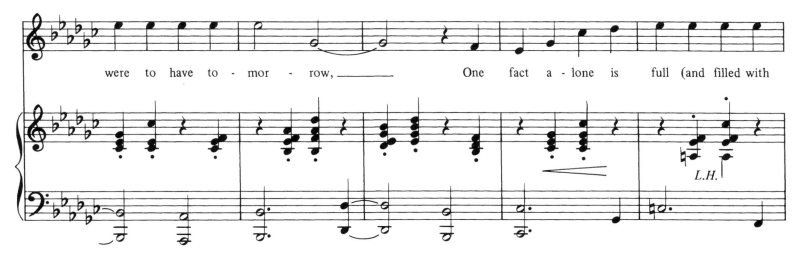

were to have to-mor-row, _____ One fact a-lone is full (and filled with

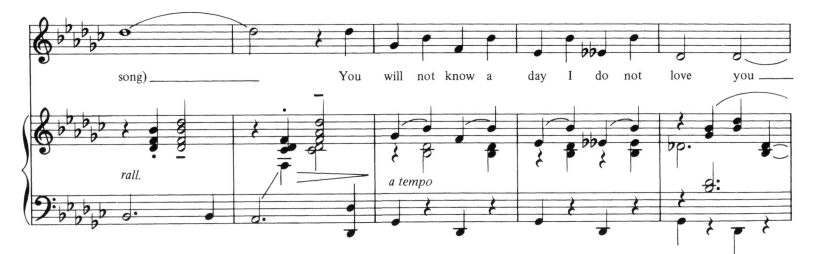

song) _____ You will not know a day I do not love you _____

_____ The way that I have loved you all a - long. _____

MY ROMANCE

JUMBO

Words by LORENZ HART
Music by RICHARD ROGERS

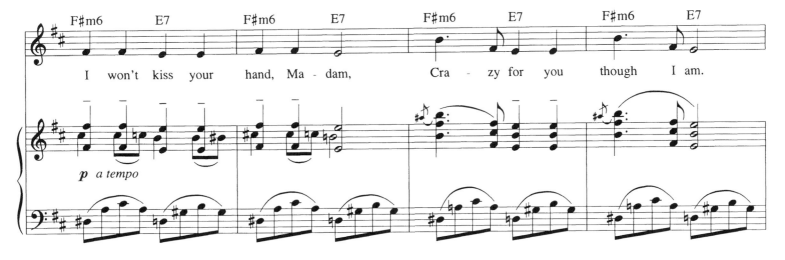

I won't kiss your hand, Ma - dam, Cra - zy for you though I am.

I'll nev - er woo you on bend - ed knee, No Ma - dam, not me.

We don't need that flow - 'ry fuss, No sir, Ma - dam, not for us.

Refrain (smoothly with expression)

My ro - mance does - n't have to have a moon in the sky, My ro -
mance does - n't need a blue la - goon stand - ing by; No month of
May, no twin - kling stars, no hide a - way, no
soft gui - tars. My ro - mance does - n't need a cas - tle

ris - ing in Spain, Nor a dance to a con-stant-ly sur -

pris - ing re-frain. Wide a - wake I can make my most fan -

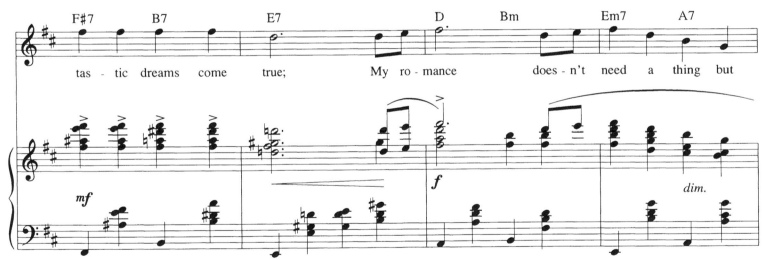

tas - tic dreams come true; My ro - mance does-n't need a thing but

you. My ro - you.

KANSAS CITY
OKLAHOMA!

Lyrics by OSCAR HAMMERSTEIN II
Music by RICHARD RODGERS

whut the mod - ren world was com - in' to! _____ I

count - ed twen - ty gas bug - gies go - in' by their - sel's

Al - most ev - 'ry time I tuck a walk _____

'Nen I put my ear to a Bell Tel - e - phone And a

strange wom - ern start - ed in to talk! _____

Refrain

Ev - 'ry-thin's up to date in Kan - sas Cit - y _____ They've
Ev - 'ry-thin's up to date in Kan - sas Cit - y _____ They've

gone a - bout as fur as they c'n go! _____ They
gone a - bout as fur as they c'n go! _____ They

went and built a sky - scrap - er sev - en stor - ies
got a big the - ay - ter they call a bur - lee -

high _____ A - bout as high as a build - in' ort - a
que _____ Fer fif - ty cents you c'n see a dand - y

grow. Ev - 'ry - thin's like a dream in Kan - sas
show. One of the gals was fat and pink and

Cit - y _____ It's bet - ter than a
pret - ty _____ As round a - bove as

mag - ic lan - tern show! _____ Y' c'n
she was round be - low. _____ I could

turn the rad - i - a - tor on when - ev - er you want some
swear that she was pad - ded from her should - er to her

heat _____ With ev - 'ry kind o' com - fort ev - 'ry
heel _____ But lat - er in the sec - ond act when

house is all com - plete. _____ You c'n walk to priv - ies
she be - gun to peel _____ She proved that ev - 'ry -

in the rain and nev - er wet your feet! They've
thin' she had and was ab - so - lute - ly real! She

gone a - bout as fur as they c'n go! They've
went a - bout as fur as she could go! She

1.

gone a - bout as fur as they c'n go!
went a - bout as fur as she could

2.

go!

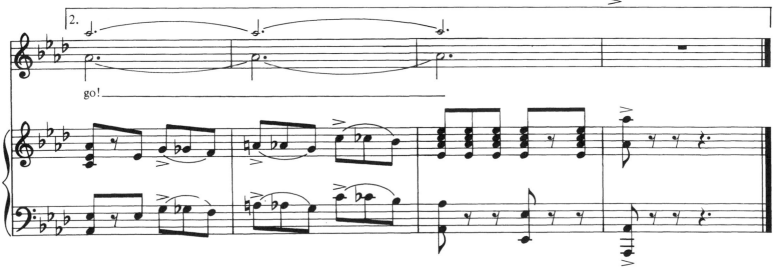

A MAN AND A WOMAN

110 IN THE SHADE

Words by TOM JONES
Music by HARVEY SCHMIDT

Andantino

Refrain (slowly with feeling)

A man and a wom-an can be so close to-geth-er that they

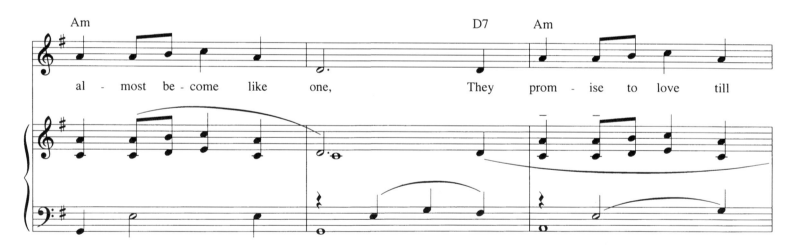

al - most be - come like one, They prom - ise to love till

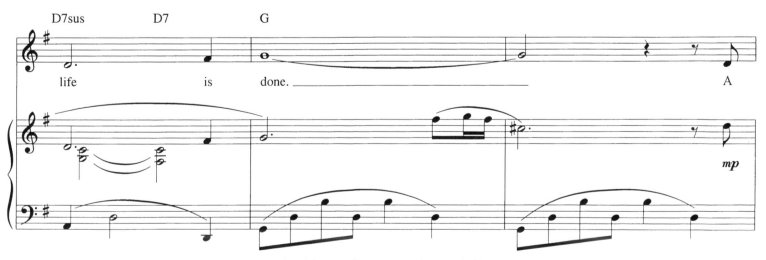

life is done. _____

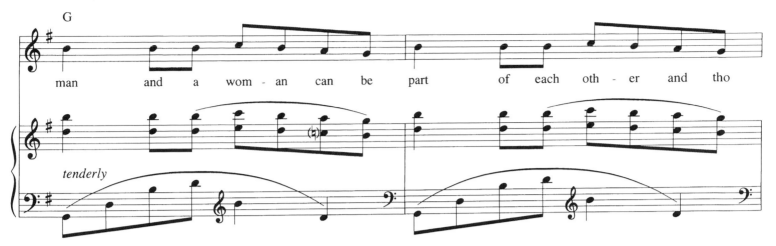

man and a wom - an can be part of each oth - er and tho

tenderly

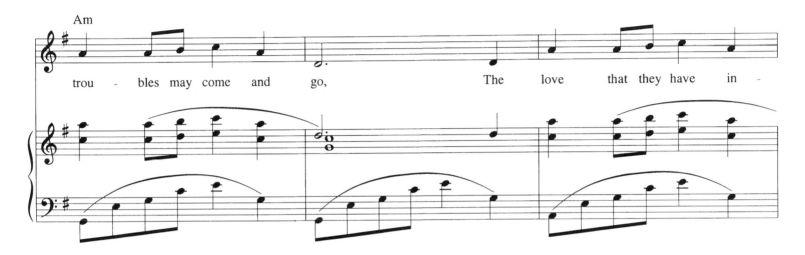

trou - bles may come and go, The love that they have in -

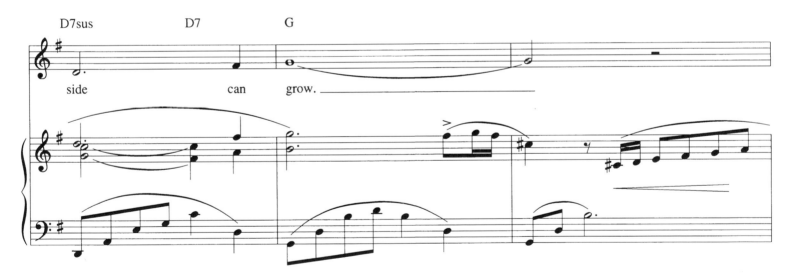

side can grow.

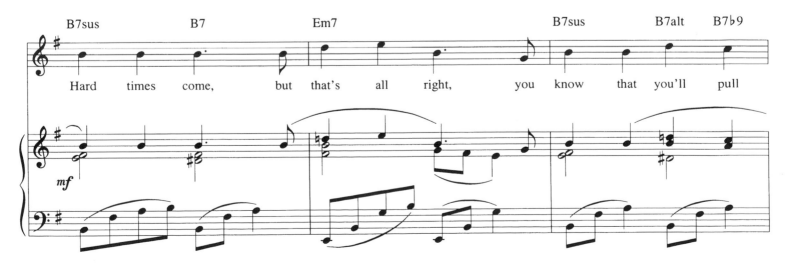

Hard times come, but that's all right, you know that you'll pull

Em   Em7   A7   Dmaj7

thru;   As long as you have each oth - er,   there's

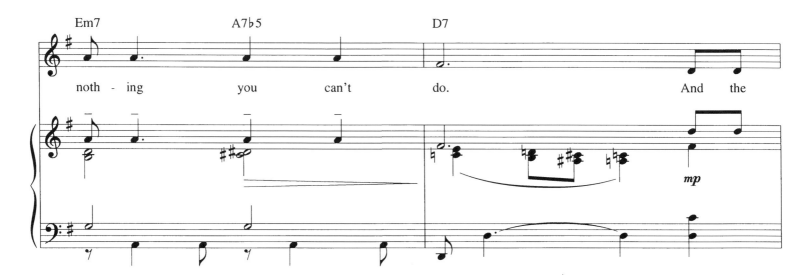

Em7   A7♭5   D7

noth - ing you can't do.   And the

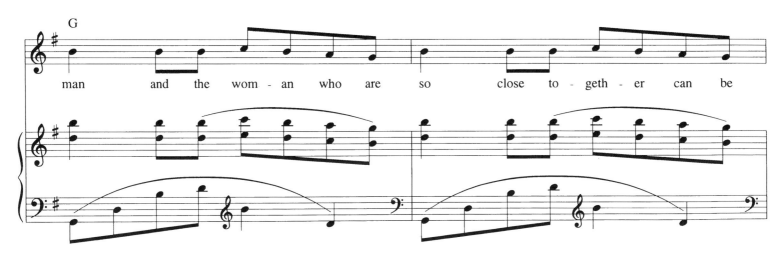

G

man   and the wom - an who are so   close to - geth - er can be

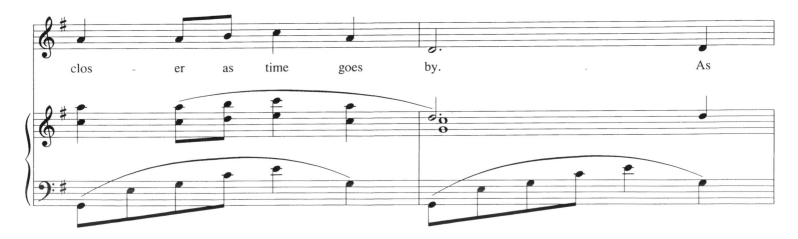

clos - er as time goes by.   As

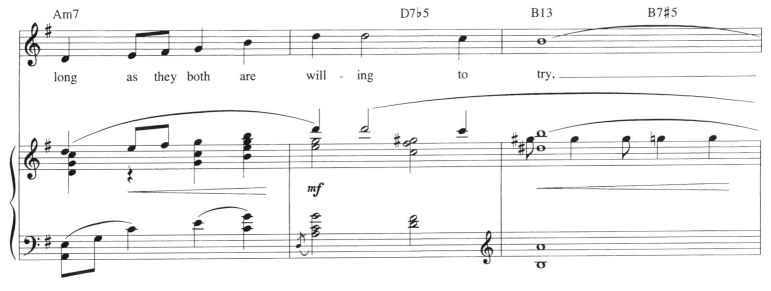

long as they both are will - ing to try,

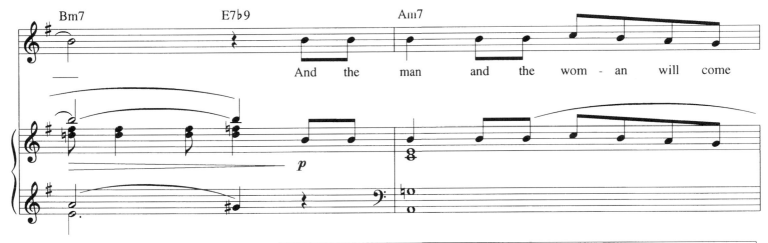

And the man and the wom - an will come

clos - er un - til the day they die. _____ A

die. _____

ME AND MY GIRL

ME AND MY GIRL

Words by DOUGLAS FURBER and ARTHUR ROSE
Music by NOEL GAY

MY HEART STOOD STILL

A CONNECTICUT YANKEE

Words by LORENZ HART
Music by RICHARD RODGERS

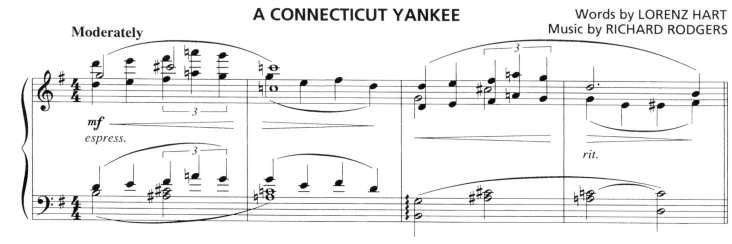

I laughed at sweet-hearts I met at schools; All in-dis-creet hearts

Seemed ro-man-tic fools. A house in

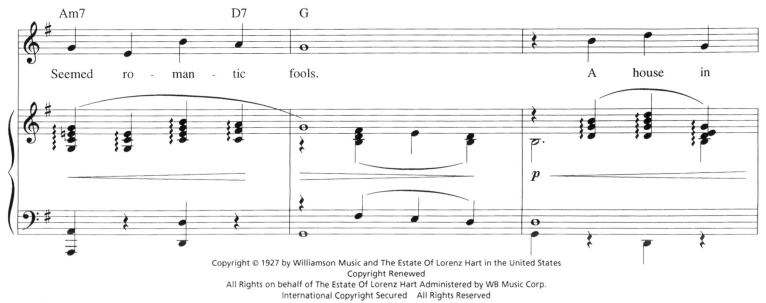

Ice - land Was my heart's do - main. I

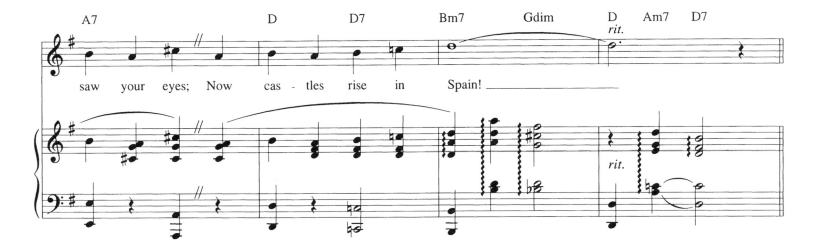

saw your eyes; Now cas - tles rise in Spain! _____

Refrain (slow but liltingly)

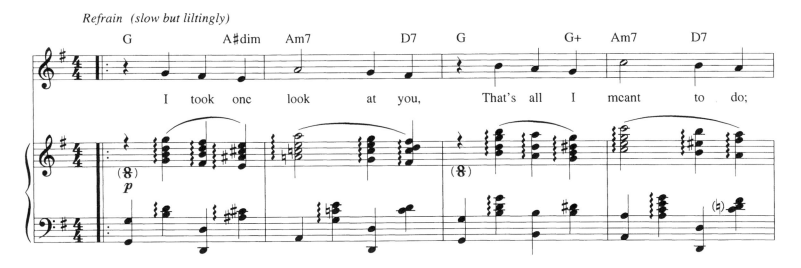

I took one look at you, That's all I meant to do;

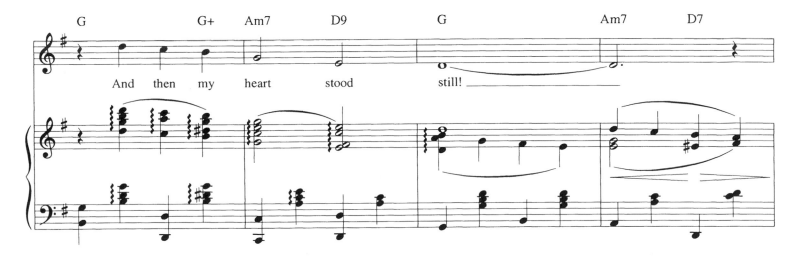

And then my heart stood still! _____

40

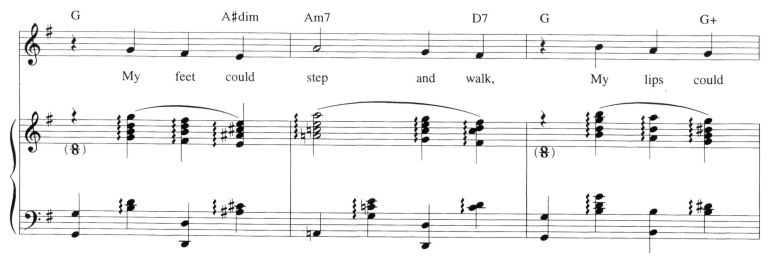

My feet could step and walk, My lips could

move and talk, And yet my heart stood

still! _____ Though not a sin-gle word was

spok-en, I could tell you knew, _____ That un-felt

clasp of hands ___ Told me so well you knew. ___

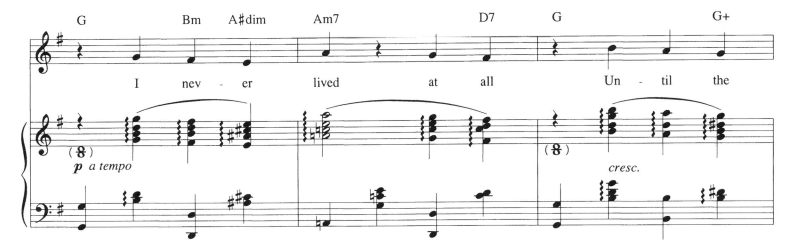

I nev-er lived at all Un - til the

thrill of that mo - ment when my heart stood

still. still. ___

OH, WHAT A BEAUTIFUL MORNIN'
OKLAHOMA!

Lyrics by OSCAR HAMMERSTEIN II
Music by RICHARD RODGERS

bright gold-en haze on the mead-ow, _____
cat-tle are stand-in' like stat-ues, _____
sounds of the earth are like mu-sic, _____

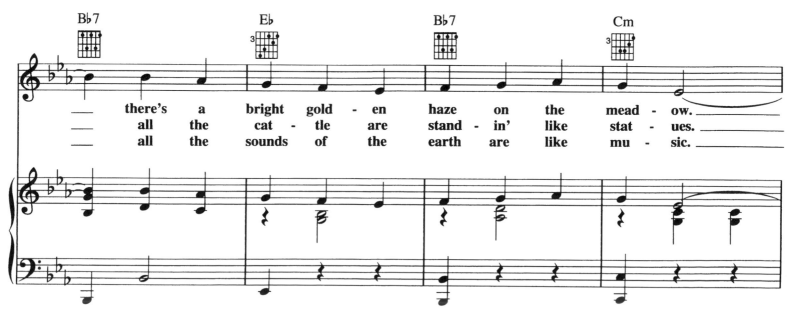

_____ there's a bright gold-en haze on the mead-ow. _____
_____ all the cat-tle are stand-in' like stat-ues. _____
_____ all the sounds of the earth are like mu-sic. _____

THE ONLY HOME I KNOW
SHENANDOAH

Lyric by PETER UDELL
Music by GARY GELD

This song is sung with chorus in the show.

pen - ny in a wish - ing well, cop - per turn - ed rust. I can't re - mem - ber why I left or

what I hoped to find. I on - ly know that more and more I'm back there in my mind. ____ A

fire - place, a gen - tle face, a warm and friend - ly glow. ____ Please let it be the way it was, The

on - ly home I know. The on - ly home I know. ____

OLD DEVIL MOON
FINIAN'S RAINBOW

Words by E.Y. HARBURG
Music by BURTON LANE

that you stole from the skies. ___ It's that Old Dev-il Moon ___

in your eyes, ___ You and your glance ___ make this ro-mance ___

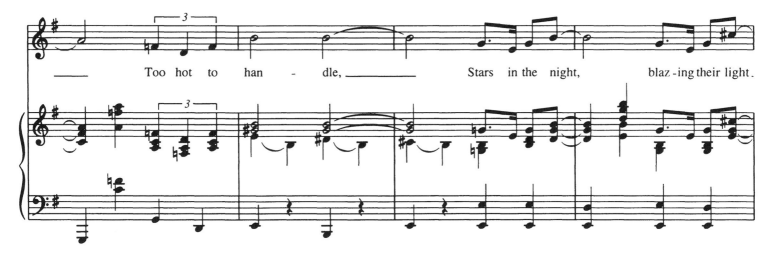

Too hot to han - dle, _____ Stars in the night, blaz-ing their light.

Can't hold a can - dle _____ to your raz - zle daz - zle. You've

got me fly - in' high and wide   On a mag - ic car - pet ride,

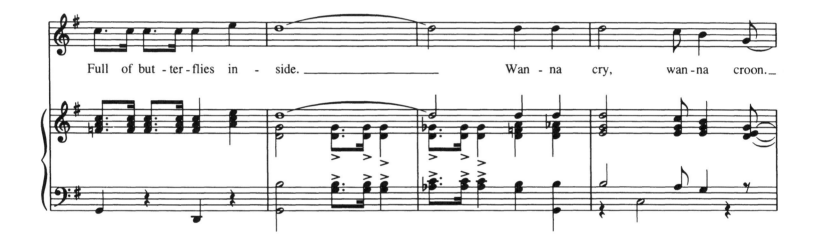

Full of but - ter - flies in - side. _____   Wan - na cry, wan - na croon. __

____ Wan - na laugh like a loon. __   It's that Old   Dev - il Moon __

in your eyes. _____ Just when I think I'm _____

free as a dove, _____ Old Dev - il Moon, deep in your

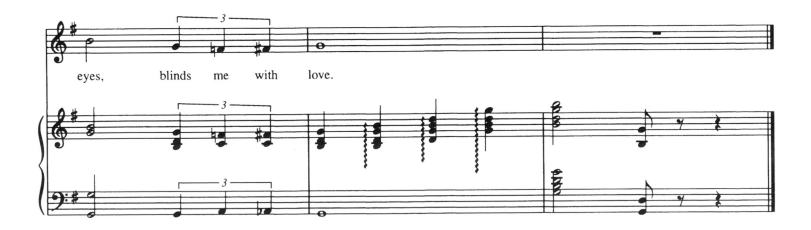

eyes, blinds me with love.

ON THE STREET WHERE YOU LIVE

MY FAIR LADY

Words by ALAN JAY LERNER
Music by FREDERICK LOEWE

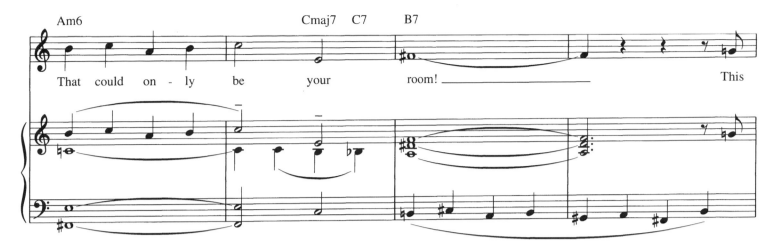

That could on-ly be your room! _____ This

street is like a gar-den and your door a gar-den gate, What a

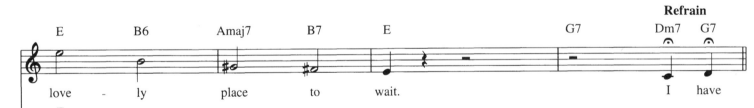

Refrain

love - ly place to wait. I have

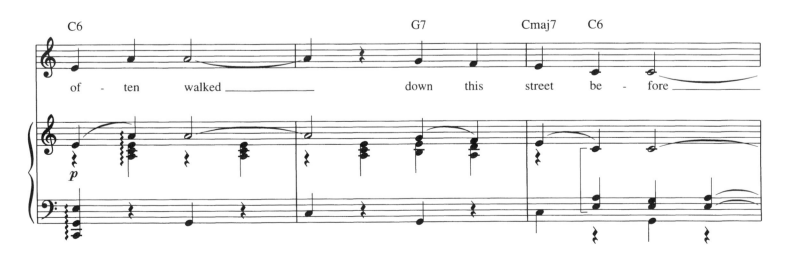

of-ten walked _____ down this street be - fore _____

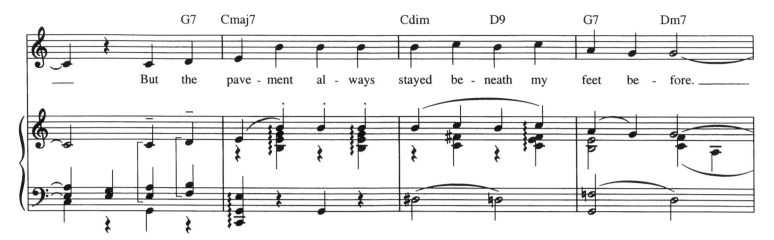

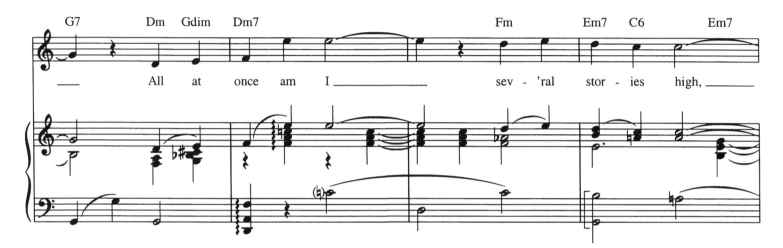

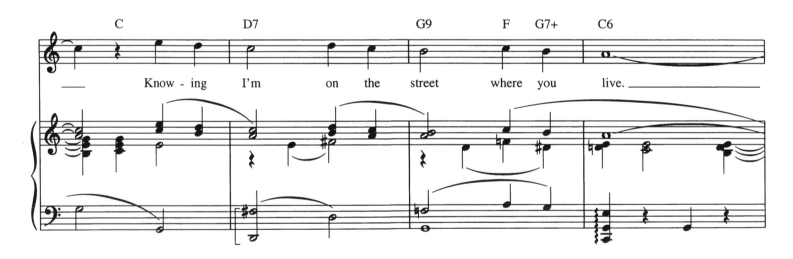

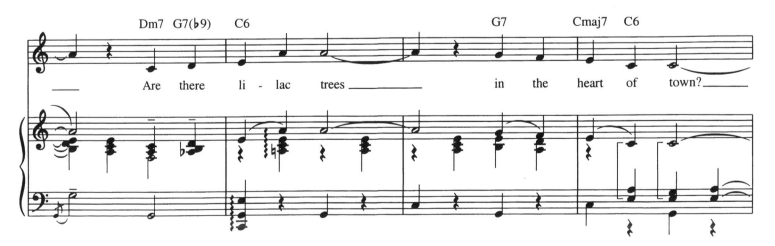

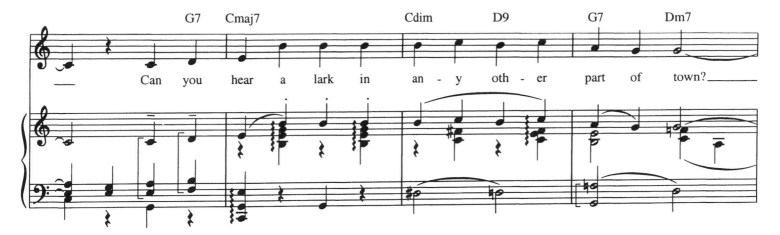

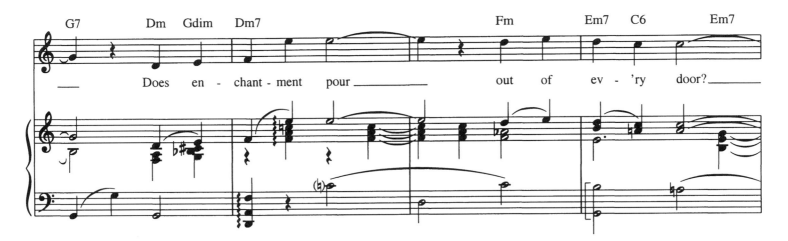

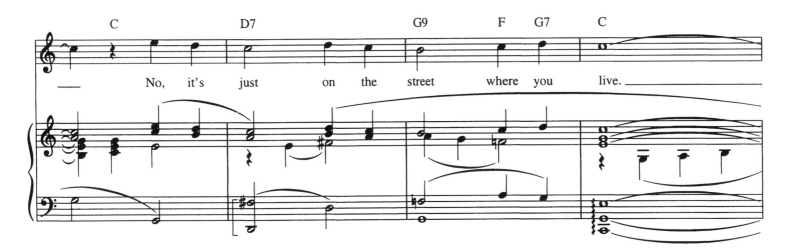

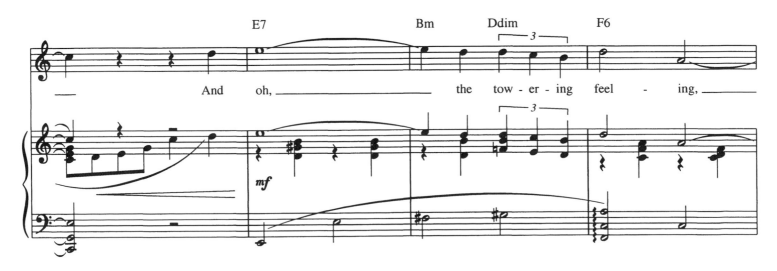

Just to know _____ some-how you are near! _____

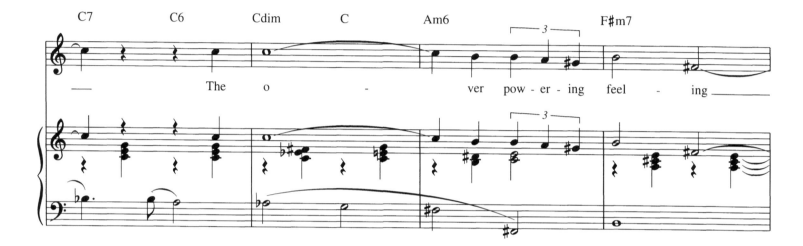

The o - ver pow-er-ing feel - ing _____

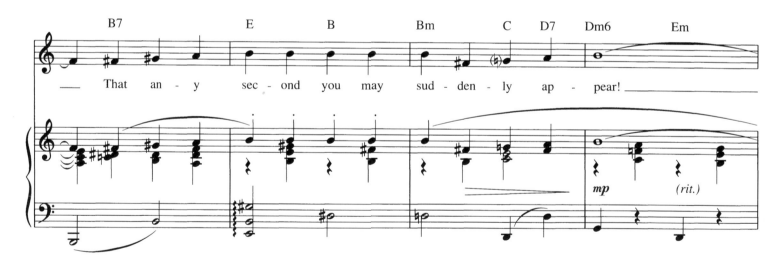

That an - y sec - ond you may sud-den-ly ap - pear! _____

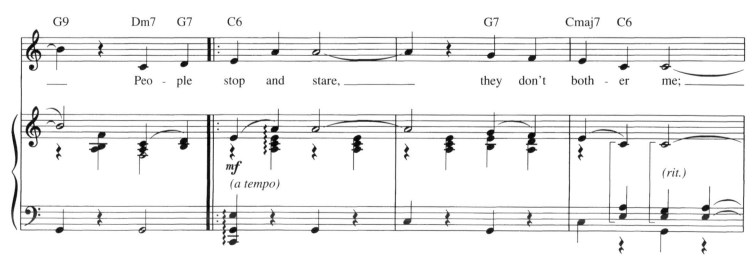

Peo - ple stop and stare, _____ they don't both - er me;

ONCE IN LOVE WITH AMY

WHERE'S CHARLEY?

By FRANK LOESSER

Slow and easy soft shoe

Verse

I caught you, sir, hav-ing a look at her As she went stroll-ing

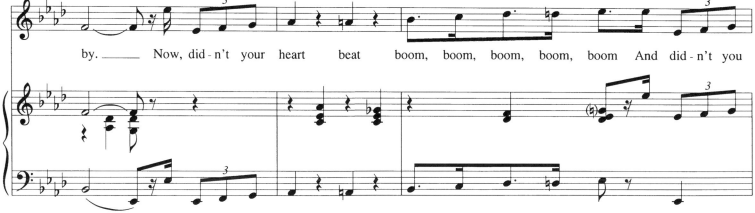

by. _____ Now, did-n't your heart beat boom, boom, boom, boom, boom And did-n't you

sigh a sigh? I warn you, sir, don't start to dream of her. Just

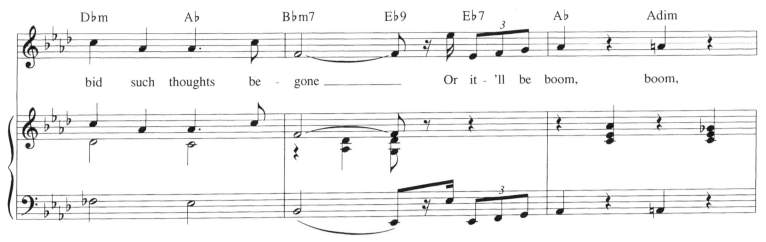

bid such thoughts be - gone _____ Or it - 'll be boom, boom,

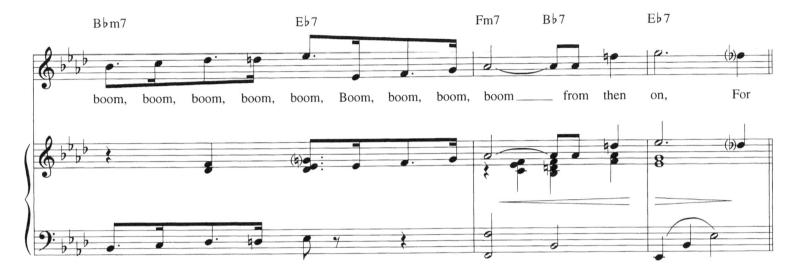

boom, boom, boom, boom, boom, Boom, boom, boom, boom _____ from then on, For

Chorus

Once in love with A-my, __ Al-ways in love with A-my. __

Ev-er and ev-er fas-cin-at-ed by 'er, Sets your heart a-fire __ to stay.

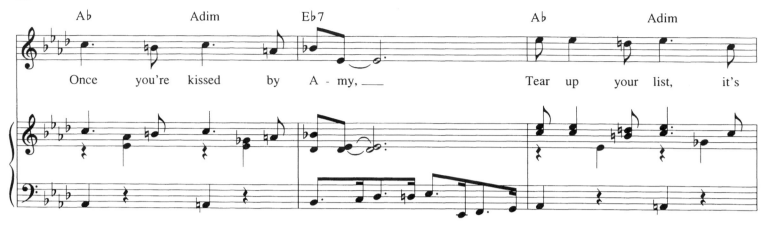

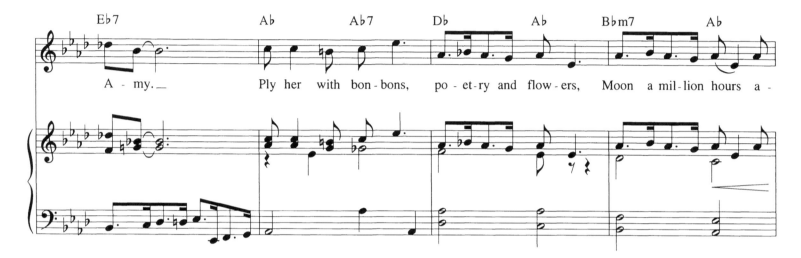

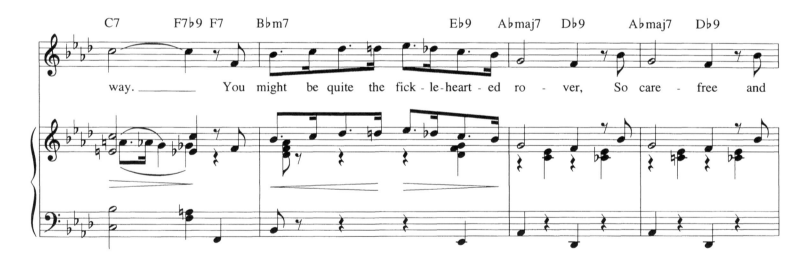

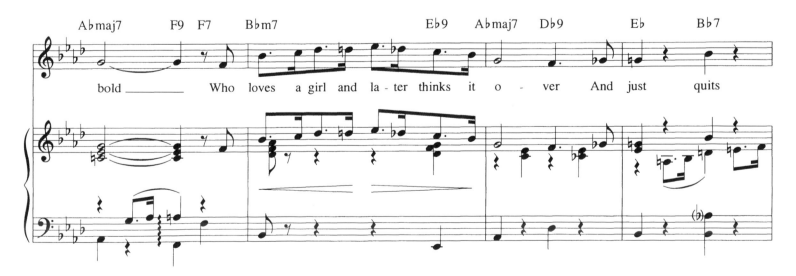

cold, But once in love with A - my, ___ Al - ways in love with

A - my. ___ Ev - er and ev - er sweet - ly you'll ro - mance 'er.

Trou - ble is, the an - swer will be _____ That A - my'd rath - er stay in love with

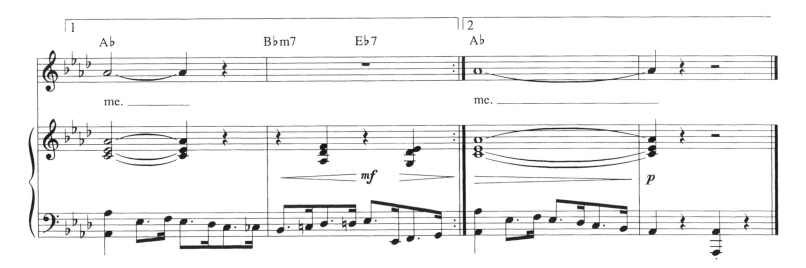

me. _____ me.

PLANT A RADISH
THE FANTASTICKS

Words by TOM JONES
Music by HARVEY SCHMIDT

know un - til the seed is near - ly grown, Just what you've sown. So
soon as you think you know what kind you've got, It's what they're not. So

plant a car - rot; get a car - rot, Not a brus - sel sprout.
plant a cab - bage; get a cab - bage, Not a sau - er - kraut.

That's why I love veg - 'ta - bles, You know what you're a - bout!
That's why I love veg - 'ta - bles, You know what you're a - bout!

Life is mer - ry if it's ver - y veg - e - tar - i - an. A
Life is mer - ry if it's ver - y veg - e - tar - i - an. A

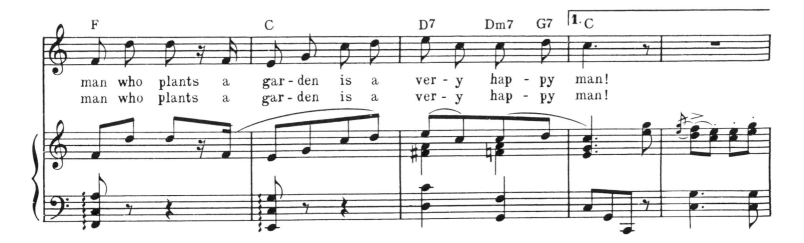

man who plants a gar-den is a ver-y hap-py man!
man who plants a gar-den is a ver-y hap-py man!

man. A veg-e-tar-i-

ver-y mer-ry veg-e-tar-

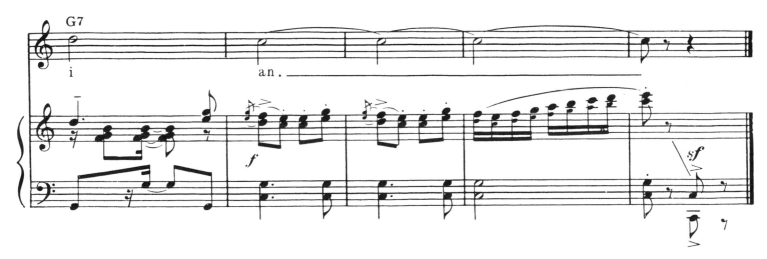

i an.

STRANGER IN PARADISE

KISMET

Words and Music by ROBERT WRIGHT
and GEORGE FORREST
(Music Based on Themes of A. Borodin)

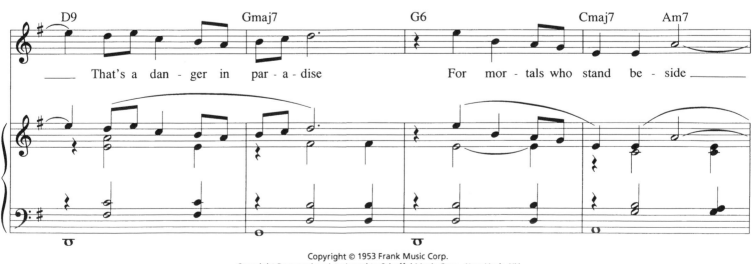

YOU'VE GOT TO BE CAREFULLY TAUGHT

SOUTH PACIFIC

Lyrics by OSCAR HAMMERSTEIN II
Music by RICHARD RODGERS

Allegro con spirito

You've got to be taught to hate and fear. You've

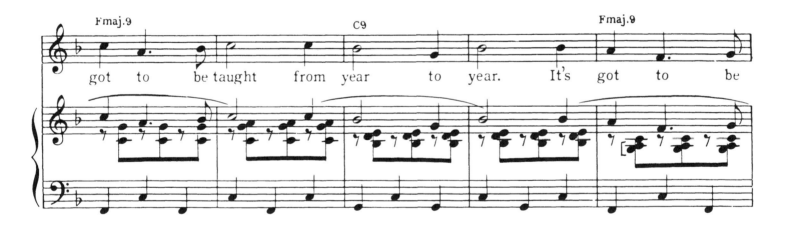

got to be taught from year to year. It's got to be

drummed in your dear lit-tle ear. You've got to be care-ful-ly

taught._____ You've got to be taught to be a-

fraid Of peo-ple whose eyes are odd - ly made, And

peo-ple whose skin is a dif - f'rent shade, You've

got to be care-ful - ly taught._____ You've

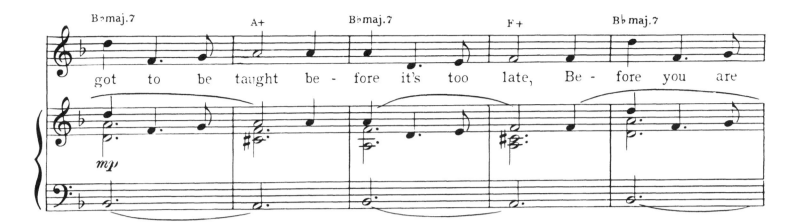

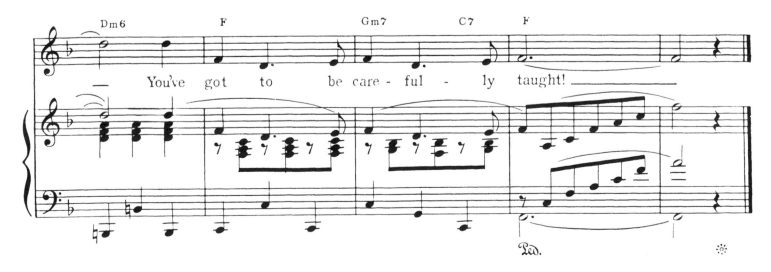

THAT'S THE WAY IT HAPPENS
ME AND JULIET

Lyrics by OSCAR HAMMERSTEIN II
Music by RICHARD RODGERS

LARRY:

You're a guy in New Hav-en on the

road with a show. There's a girl in the comp'-ny that you

hard-ly know. You watch her and you won-der if she'd like to par-take_ Of

French fried po - ta - toes and a T bone steak._

Then a - long comes a fel - low who is quick - er than you, And he

does what you thought that you would like to do._ He takes her to a bis - tro where they

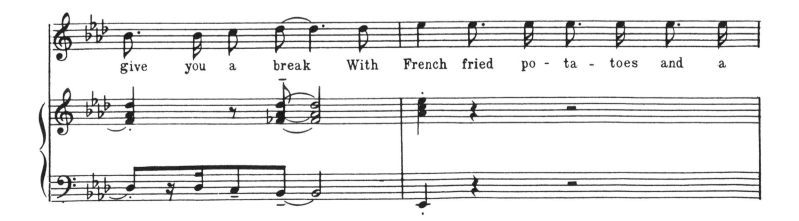

give you a break With French fried po - ta - toes and a

quasi recitando

T bone steak. Now you see them to-geth-er and you know in your heart That you lost what you want-ed from the ver-y start, Be - cause you did - n't ask her if she'd like to par-take_ Of

f

pp colla voce

colla voce

rall.

Tempo I°
(in rhythm)

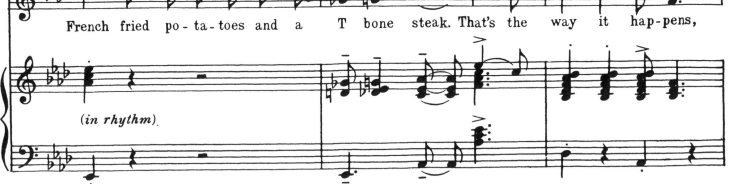

French fried po-ta-toes and a T bone steak. That's the way it hap-pens,

(in rhythm)

That's the way it hap-pens,   That's the

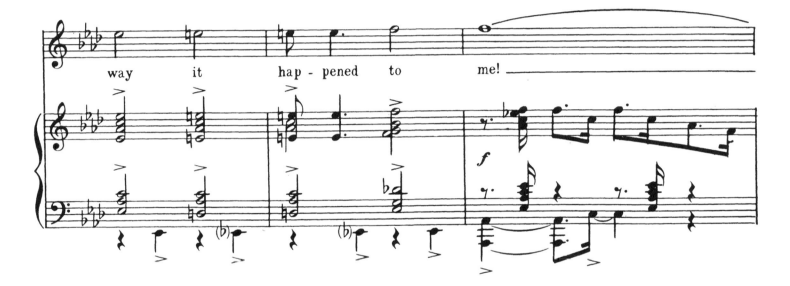

way it hap-pened to me!

VERY SOFT SHOES

ONCE UPON A MATTRESS

Music by MARY RODGERS
Words by MARSHALL BARER

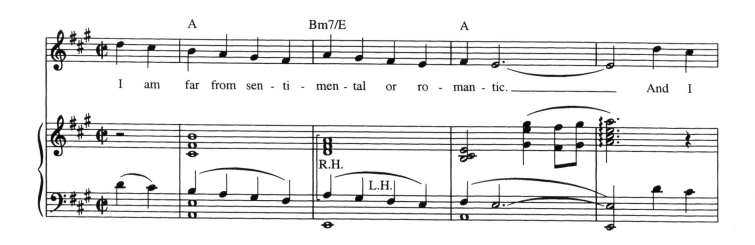

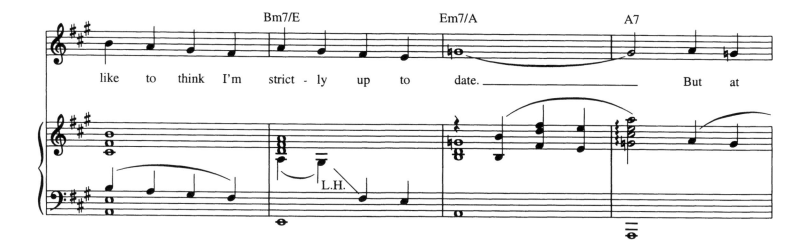

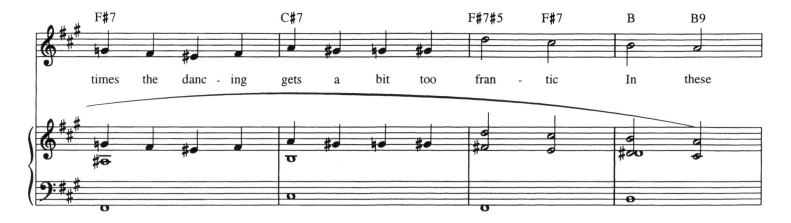

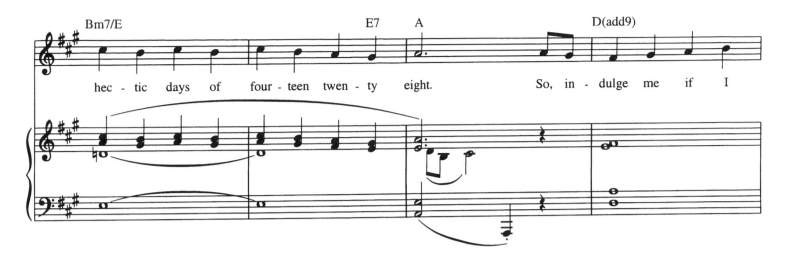

Bm7/E — E7 — A — D(add9)

hec - tic days of four - teen twen - ty eight. So, in - dulge me if I

E7 — A — D(add9)

pause to raise my chal - ice. To a quaint and charm - ing

Bm7/E — A7 — D(add9)

dance they used to do. _____ In the days when my dear

poco allarg.

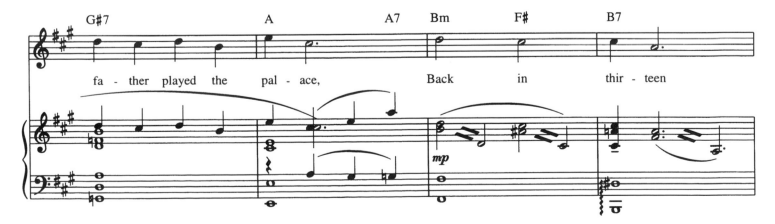

G#7 — A — A7 — Bm — F# — B7

fa - ther played the pal - ace, Back in thir - teen

mp

Moderate 4

nine - ty two. My Dad was deb - o - nair, And quite as light as air

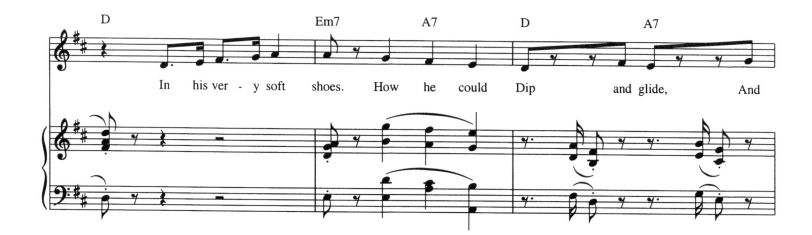

In his ver - y soft shoes. How he could Dip and glide, And

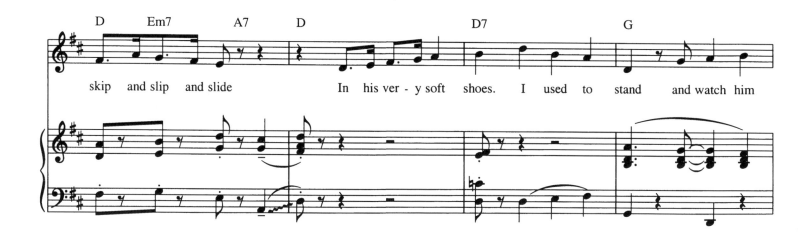

skip and slip and slide In his ver - y soft shoes. I used to stand and watch him

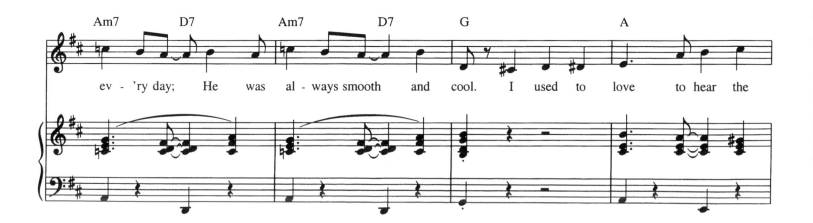

ev - 'ry day; He was al - ways smooth and cool. I used to love to hear the

peo - ple say: _ He's a reg - u - lar danc - ing fool. He bare - ly Touched the ground And

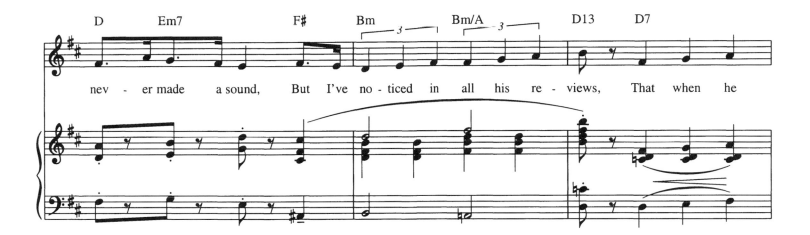

nev - er made a sound, But I've no - ticed in all his re - views, That when he

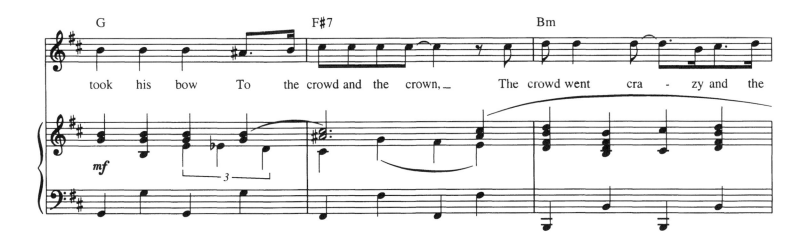

took his bow To the crowd and the crown, _ The crowd went cra - zy and the

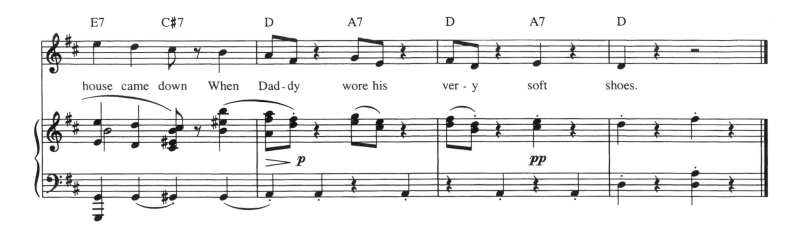

house came down When Dad - dy wore his ver - y soft shoes.

WE KISS IN A SHADOW

THE KING AND I

Lyrics by OSCAR HAMMERSTEIN II
Music by RICHARD ROGERS

Molto moderato e semplice

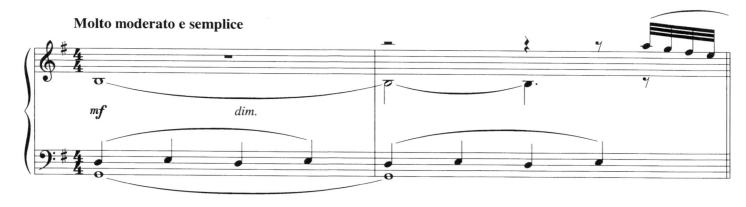

Refrain (slowly and tenderly)

We kiss in a sha - dow

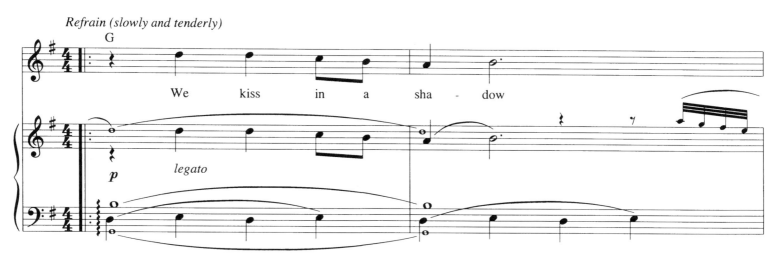

We hide from the moon,

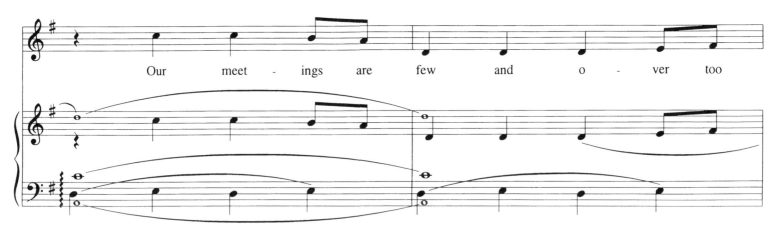

Our meet - ings are few and o - ver too

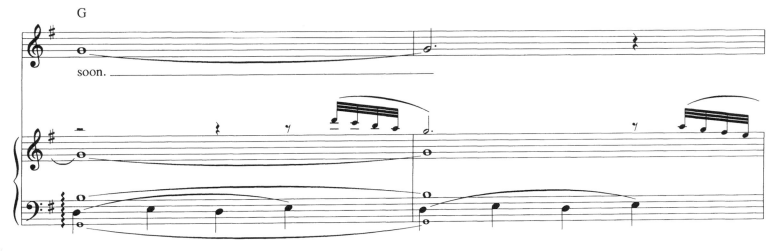

soon. _____

We speak in a whis - per, A - fraid to be

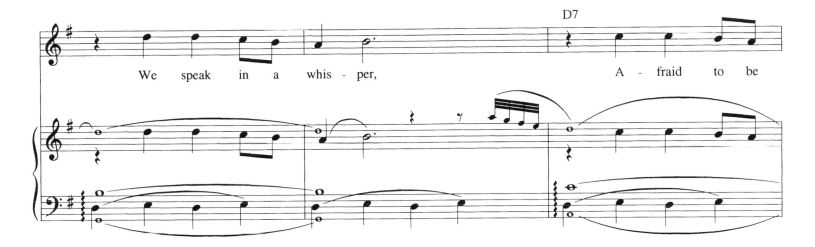

heard; When peo - ple are near, we speak not a

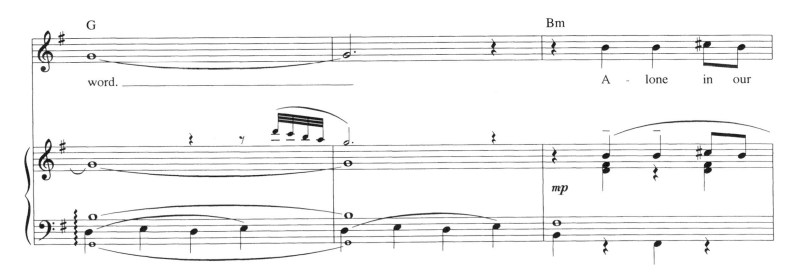

word. _____ A - lone in our

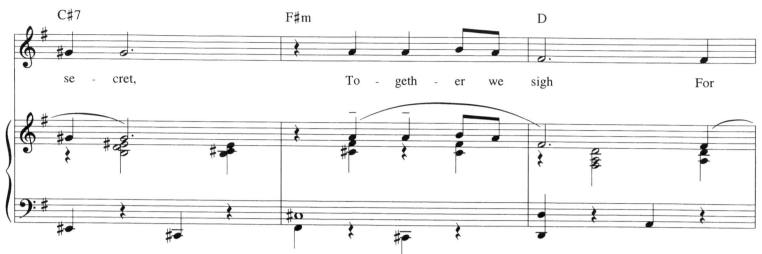

se - cret, To - geth - er we sigh For

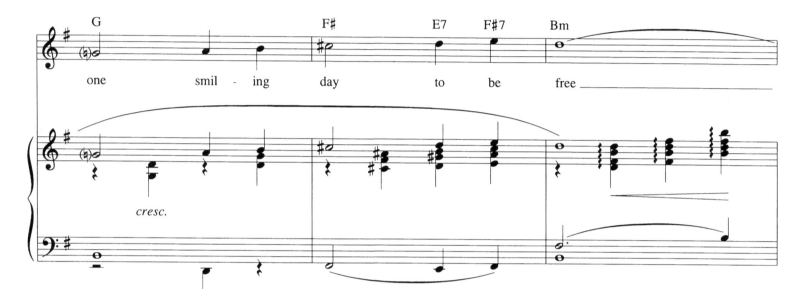

one smil - ing day to be free _____

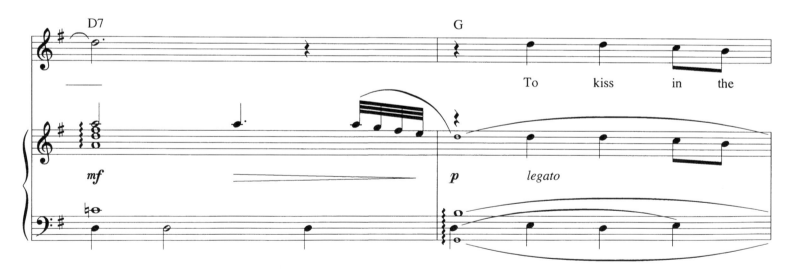

To kiss in the

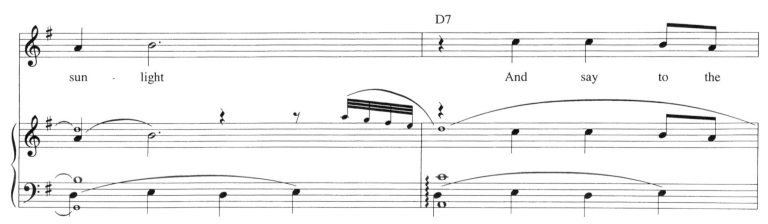

sun - light And say to the

sky _____ Be - hold and be - lieve what you

see! _____ Be - hold how my

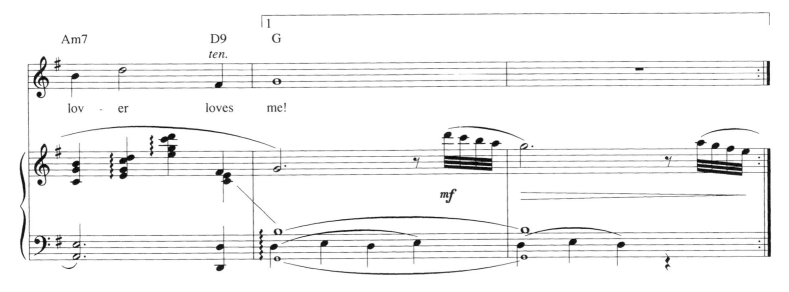

lov - er loves me!

me! _____

WHEN THE CHILDREN ARE ASLEEP

CAROUSEL

Lyrics by OSCAR HAMMERSTEIN II
Music by RICHARD RODGERS

tip - toe in - to our sit - tin' room, where we love to be by our -

selves, Where the flick - rin' glow of the fi - re - light makes the

books wink down from their shelves. And there ev - 'ry eve - nin', we'll

al - ways be, Me in my arm - chair, You on my knee.

Refrain

When the chil-dren are a-sleep, we'll sit and dream _____

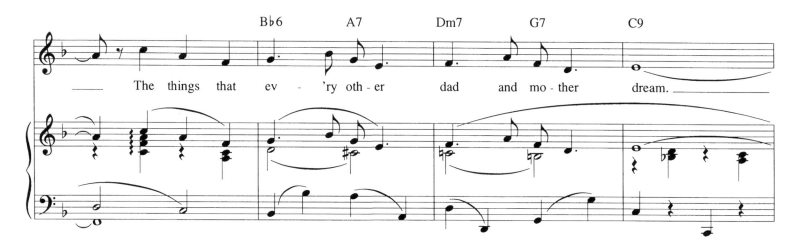

_____ The things that ev - 'ry oth-er dad and mo-ther dream. _____

_____ When the chil-dren are a-sleep and lights are low, _____

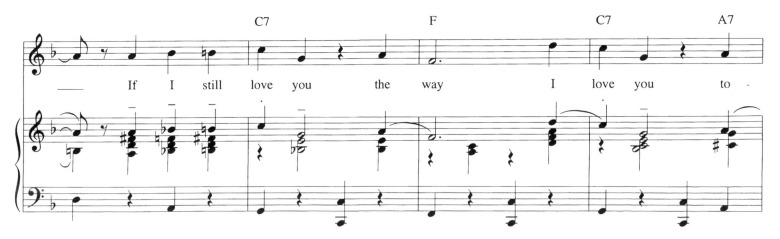

_____ If I still love you the way I love you to -

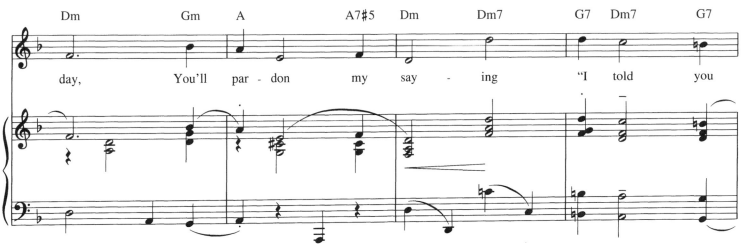

day, You'll par-don my say-ing "I told you

so!" When the chil-dren are a-sleep, I'll dream with

you _____ We'll think what fun we have had and be

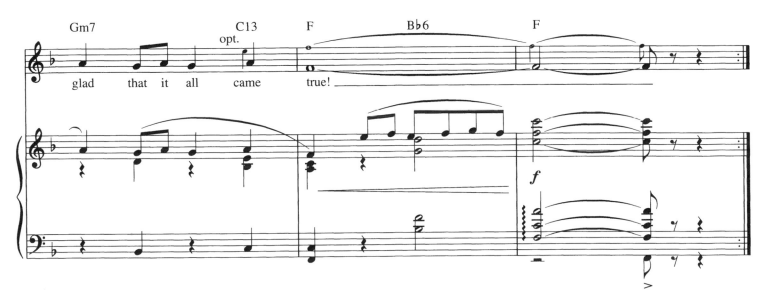

glad that it all came true! _____

A WONDERFUL DAY LIKE TODAY

THE ROAR OF THE GREASEPAINT - THE SMELL OF THE CROWD

Words and Music by LESLIE BRICUSSE
and ANTHONY NEWLEY

On a

won - der - ful day ___ like to - day, ___ I de -
won - der - ful morn - ing like this, ___ When the

fy an - y cloud ___ to ap - pear in the sky. ___
sun is as big ___ as a yel - low bal - loon. ___

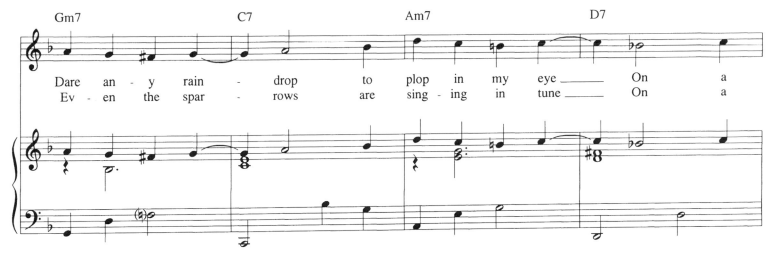

Gm7 · C7 · Am7 · D7

Dare an - y rain - drop to plop in my eye _____ On a
Ev - en the spar - rows are sing - ing in tune _____ On

Gm7 · G7 · Csus · C7

[1]

won - der - ful day _____ like to - day. _____ On a
won - der - ful morn -

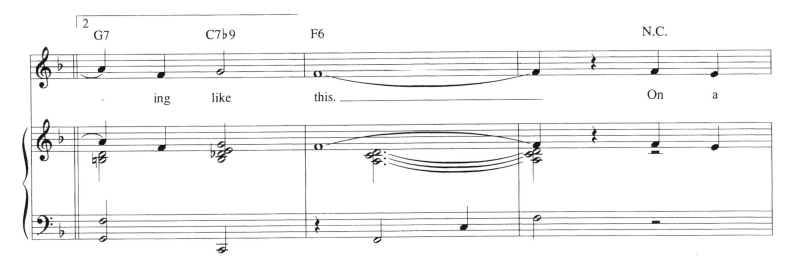

[2]

G7 · C7b9 · F6 · N.C.

- ing like this. _____ On a

Bb · Bb+ · Gm/Bb · C7/Bb

morn - ing like this _____ I could kiss ev - 'ry - bod - y I'm

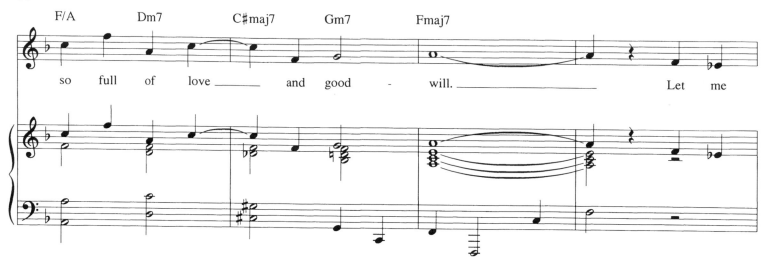

so full of love _____ and good - will. _____ Let me

say fur - ther - more _____ I'd a - dore ev - 'ry - bod - y to

come and dine. The plea - sure's mine, And I will pay the bill. May I

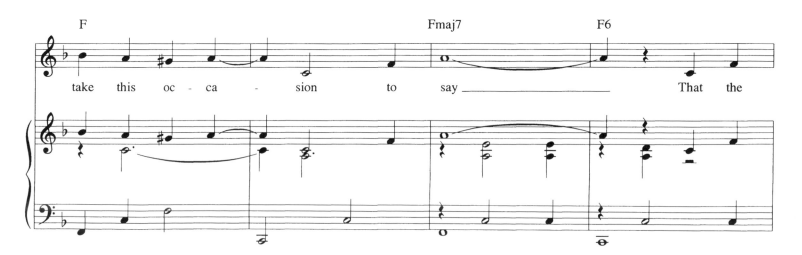

take this oc - ca - sion to say _____ That the

whole hu - man race ____ should go down on its knees, ____

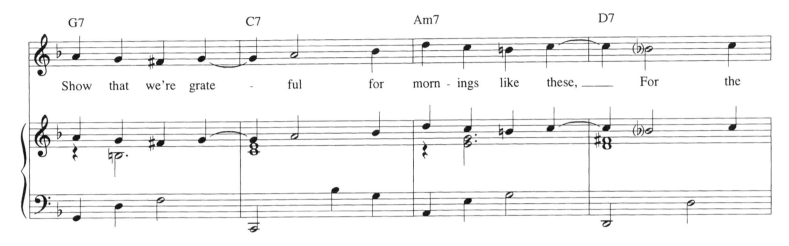

Show that we're grate - ful for morn - ings like these, ____ For the

world's in a won - der - ful way, _____ On a

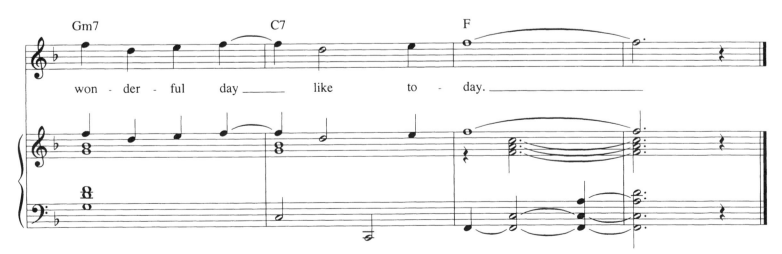

won - der - ful day ____ like to - day. ____

YOUNGER THAN SPRINGTIME

SOUTH PACIFIC

Lyrics by OSCAR HAMMERSTEIN II
Music by RICHARD RODGERS

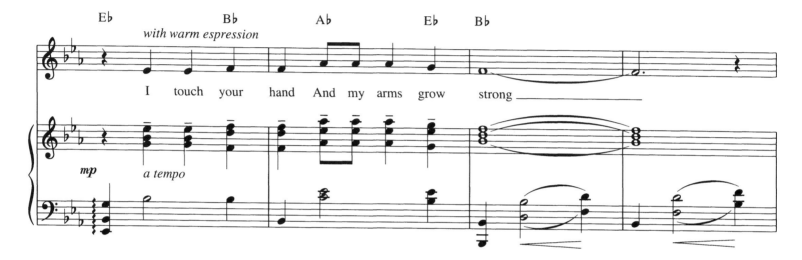

I touch your hand And my arms grow strong _____

Like a pair of birds That burst with song. _____

My eyes look down At your love - ly face _____ And I hold the

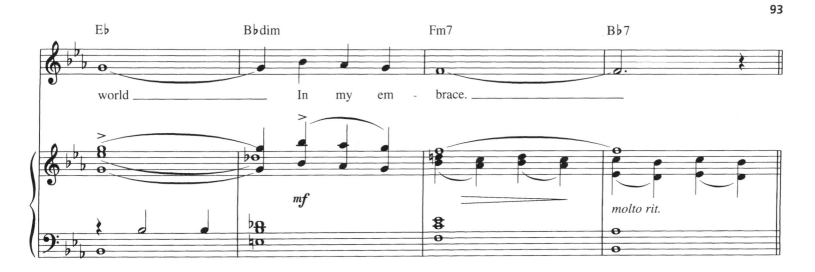

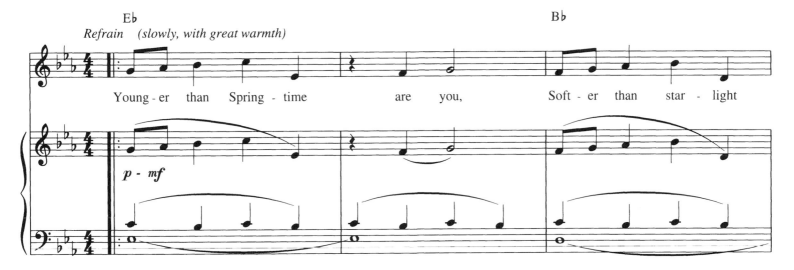

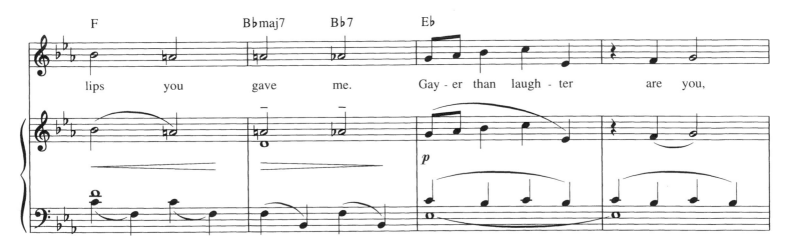

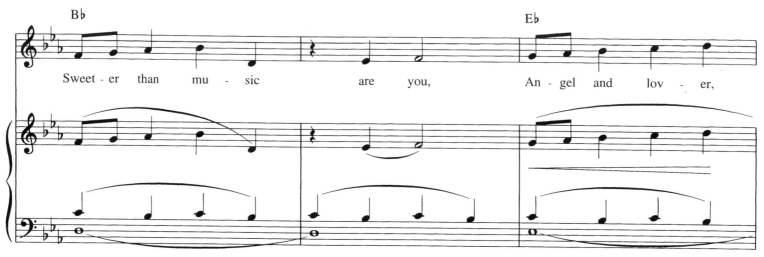

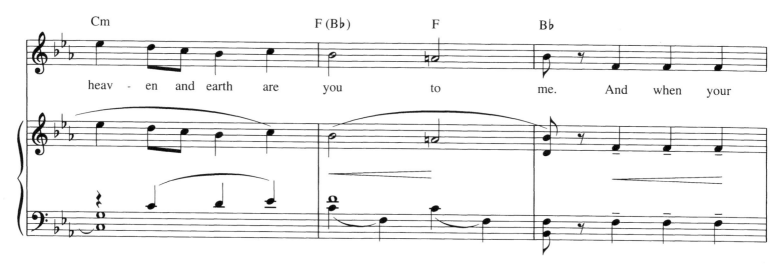

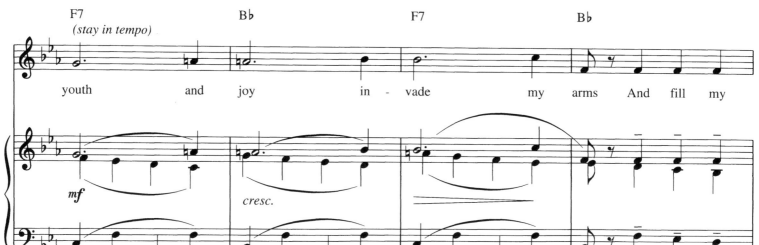

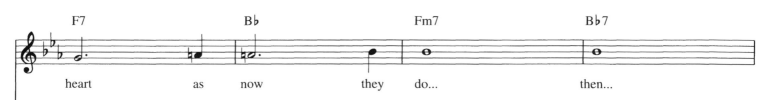

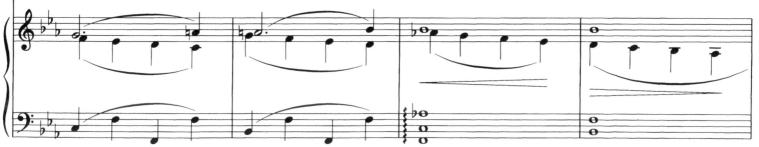

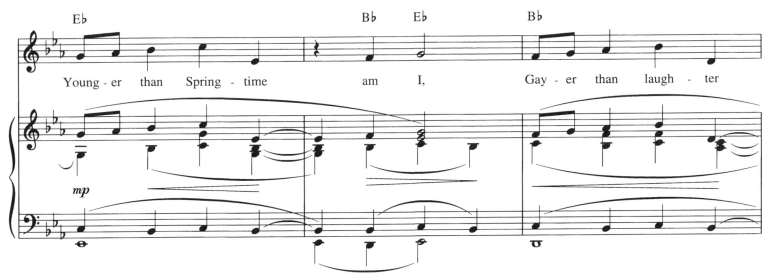

Young - er than Spring - time am I, Gay - er than laugh - ter

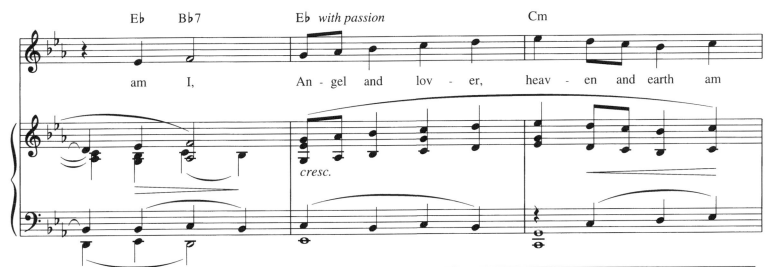

am I, An - gel and lov - er, heav - en and earth am

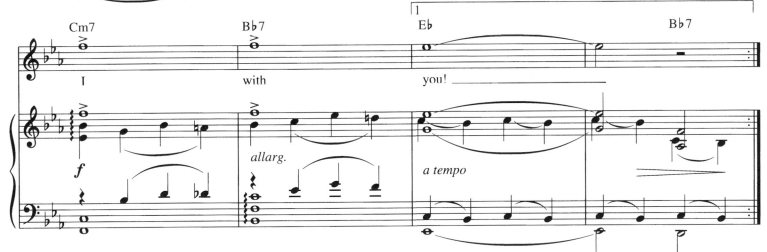

I with you!

you!